To Be A Ghost

Other books compiled by Raymond Wilson

NINE O'CLOCK BELL
OUT AND ABOUT: Poems of the Outdoors
EVERY POEM TELLS A STORY

To Be A Ghost

*Poems of Magic, Mystery and
the Supernatural*

Raymond Wilson

Illustrated by Alan Rowe

VIKING

VIKING

Published by the Penguin Group
Penguin Books Ltd, 27 Wrights Lane, London W8 5TZ, England
Penguin Books USA Inc., 375 Hudson Street, New York, New York 10014, USA
Penguin Books Australia Ltd, Ringwood, Victoria, Australia
Penguin Books Canada Ltd, 10 Alcorn Avenue, Toronto, Ontario, Canada M4V 3B2
Penguin Books (NZ) Ltd, 182–190 Wairau Road, Auckland 10, New Zealand

Penguin Books Ltd, Registered Offices: Harmondsworth, Middlesex, England

First published 1991
10 9 8 7 6 5 4 3 2 1

Filmset in Plantin (Linotron 202) by Rowland Phototypesetting Ltd, Bury St Edmunds,
Suffolk

Printed in Great Britain by Butler & Tanner Ltd, Frome, Somerset

A CIP catalogue record for this book is available from the British Library

ISBN 0–670–83695–8

Contents

To Hunt a Ghost

To hunt a ghost
it's not essential
to have an ivied ruin
(castle or monastery)
with hooting owls
and thunder growling,
though these all help.

To hunt a ghost
that is truly a ghost
what at all costs
you must guard against
are ruses, spoofs, hoaxes.

So, like a good detective,
ensure you take with you
an Instamatic camera
and tape recorder;
graphite powder,
with camel-hair brush
and magnifying glass
(for tell-tale fingerprints!);
a reel of black cotton
to stretch in strands
cordoning off exits,
chimneys and entrances;

Sellotape for windows,
and flour or starch
for sprinkling on floorboards
to highlight footmarks;
and finally,
a little luminous paint
to enable you
to pick out daubed landmarks
in the deathly dark.

Having removed each
and every possibility
of hocus-pocus,
you can rest assured
that what you've tracked down
is beyond all doubt
the authentic article –
and accordingly
you can crawl up the walls
in one hundred per cent
guaranteed genuine
TERROR!

Two's Company

(The sad story of the man who didn't believe in ghosts)

They said the house was haunted, but
He laughed at them and said, 'Tut, tut!
I've never heard such tittle-tattle
As ghosts that groan and chains that rattle;
And just to prove I'm in the right,
Please leave me here to spend the night.'

They winked absurdly, tried to smother
Their ignorant laughter, nudged each other,
And left him just as dusk was falling
With a hunchback moon and screech-owls calling.
Not that this troubled him one bit;
In fact, he was quite glad of it,
Knowing it's every sane man's mission
To contradict all superstition.

But what is that? Outside it seemed
As if chains rattled, someone screamed!
Come, come, it's merely nerves, he's certain
(But just the same, he draws the curtain).
The stroke of twelve – but there's no clock!
He shuts the door and turns the lock
(Of course, he knows that no one's there,
But no harm's done by taking care!)
Someone's outside – the silly joker,
(He may as well pick up the poker!).
That noise again! He checks the doors,
Shutters the windows, makes a pause
To seek the safest place to hide –
(The cupboard's strong – he creeps inside).
'Not that there's anything to fear,'
He tells himself, when at his ear
A voice breathes softly, 'How do you do!
I am the ghost. Pray, who are you?'

Ghost

It stood there ruefully raising both its arms and very gradually disappeared

In a Far Land

In a far land
a black mountain broods:
beneath the black mountain
stretch the green woods.

Among the green woods
a white castle soars:
in the white castle
are dark corridors.

The corridors lead
to a black, shut door.
Behind it a Prince
sprawls dead on the floor.

With a cobwebbed cup
by his withered hand,
a Prince lies poisoned
in that far land.

A hobbling old Princess
creeps to that door –
ghost calling ghost
for evermore!

She murmurs her guilt
in sighs and soft moans.
Behind the locked door
the dead Prince groans.

The Haunting

At the foot of the bed in the dead of the night
    It stood there, or rather It *hovered* –
Two luminous eyes and a face ghastly white
    From which I have never recovered.

When I asked, 'Who are you?' It looked taken aback,
    Indeed, you could say It looked frightened;
But then, *I* was too, and my hair, raven-black,
    From that moment has curiously whitened.

So I asked It once more, 'Who *are* you?' – Again
    Its pale lips moved mockingly, mutely,
While the night-wind howled loud in the sobbing rain
    And It stared back, trembling acutely.

Which seeing, I screwed up my courage and switched
    On the lamp, hands fumbling in terror –
Then my eyes met a jibbering idiot who twitched
    Like my twin in the newly hung mirror!

Hanged Man's Ghost

I never go up to the attic
    (Mum calls it her 'Guest Room'!)
and sooner than spend a night up there
    I'd choose a haunted tomb.

It's not that I mind the way the air
    turns suddenly to ice,
or even the way the floorboards groan,
    though it's not what you'd call nice.

The thing I can't stand is the shadow
    that thickens as you stare
and stains the daylight as it twirls
    suspended in mid-air.

It hangs from the beam of the rafter
    just over your head,
and it's poised like a hairy fat spider
    to drop straight on the bed.

It's bad enough in your own room
    trying hard not to shout
when a hand from outside the blankets
    seeks your own hand, dangling out;

but far, far worse in its web of shadows
    under the tall roof-top
hangs the black and bloated man-eating spider,
    just waiting to drop!

The Murdered Husband's Complaint

She shouldn't have gone and done it!
    It came as quite a blow
and was hurtful to my feelings,
    as she was bound to know,
for putting arsenic in one's tea's
    a cruel death, and slow.
Tonight I'll visit her bedside
    and I shall *tell* her so!

Happy Ghost

Joy Brightwell stood at my bedside
    and my heart seized up with fear.
'Joy Brightwell,' I said, 'don't you know you're dead
    and there's no way you should be here?'

'I thought I'd come back and take a look
    at how it used to be,'
Joy Brightwell said, 'but the whole place is dead –
    not to mention the company.'

'You were always one for a laugh, Joy –
    that is, when you were here.'
'If you want real laughter, just try the Hereafter,'
    she said, grinning from ear to ear.

'It's not so bad, then, where you are?'
    'Bad? It's not bad at all.
I tell you, it's bliss. Just you try doing this!'
    and, smiling, she stepped through the wall.

Tudor Ghosts

The learned Queen Elizabeth
has haunted, ever since her death,
far back in sixteen hundred and three,
the Windsor Castle library.
Her hair fire-red, her teeth coal-black,
she reaches books down from the rack
and reads in Latin, French and Spanish
for an hour or so – and then she'll vanish!

Her father (Henry the Eighth to you)
swaggers round making a hullabaloo
in the Deanery, where he stamps and roars
down dark and echoing corridors;
and should anyone disturb him there,
his huge bulk thins to empty air.

His second wife, Queen Anne Boleyn,
puts in an appearance now and again
up river, in the Bloody Tower,
and carries round, at midnight hour,
crowned still and coiffured, her own head,
tucked in her arm like a loaf of bread.

Meanwhile, at Hampton Court, wife three
(Jane Seymour) climbs to the Gallery,
with hand cupped round a lighted taper –
then fades and drifts away like vapour.

Nearby, Queen Catherine Howard (wife five),
though never seen, can still contrive
to scream her head off – though it may be
one shouldn't take this *literally*,
since (like wife two) she did much to tax
King Henry's nerves, and died by the axe.

(Though ghost-hunters search, no one has seen
so much as a fleeting glimpse of Queen
Catherine of Aragon's ghost so far.
Ditto Anne of Cleves and Catherine Parr.)

The Quiet Ghost

The Poltergeist's a noisy ghost
    which crashes, bangs and knocks.
There's no name for the quiet ghost
    on tiptoe, wearing socks,
that sneaks upstairs without a sound
    and can unpick the locks
and steal into your room where it
    just hangs about and shocks
with silences ten times as bad
    as crashes, bangs and knocks.

Power Cut

The night we had the power cut
    the lights went out,
    the telly went phut!
    the dog got trod on,
    Mum couldn't put
    her hand on the candles;
    Dad did his nut!

In fact, it turned out quite a night
    when finally
    we set things right
    and huddled, drawing
    the blankets tight
    around us, in flicker-
    ing candle-light.

Tom joked that what we needed most
    to round the night off
    was a spook or a ghost,
    when a smock-coated farmer
    with a beard like frost
    coughed from the corner
    and winked at his host!

You'll guess what Mum and Dad had to say
     ('It's all in your minds!'),
     but be that as it may,
     it just *doesn't* explain
     why the very next day
     we found in the corner
     a bale of fresh hay!

Phantom Coach

On March the eighth at two a.m.
the Phantom Coach emerges from
the mist-hung pond in Heron Wood
unspotted by duckweed, slime or mud.

By murky starlight, all lamps lit,
with brass and woodwork polished bright,
it hurtles like a torrent down
highway and byway and country lane.

Its headless coachman, whip in hand,
lashes his horses from behind
past cottage, manor house and farm,
where none dares breathe for fear of him.

Four times he hauls his team to rest,
four times he adds to his grim list,
then, with four passengers inside,
back to the pond, in a stampede!

Till two a.m. next eighth of March
never will come another coach
with steaming horses storming by,
all clashing hooves and white of eye!

Now You See Him . . .

The clicking of wheels had lulled me asleep
     travelling the old branch line
when I slowly came to in the dim half-light
of a railway carriage that crawled through a night
     as dark as a disused mine.

And there in the corner seat opposite
     he sat with a startled smile;
then he chatted about one thing and another
as if I'd been his long-lost brother,
     for mile upon weary mile.

But just as my eyes grew leaden again
     all sleep was abruptly banished
by his voice pleading, '*Tell me you're not a ghost*!' –
which I did, and was trying my uttermost
     to convince him so when he vanished!

Herne the Hunter

When the whistling winds of winter strip Windsor
                                                    Forest bare,
   And soft snow falls where the dark wood sprawls,
   And the wandering screech-owl hoots and calls
           On the freezing air,
A wild-eyed horseman will hunt you down, if you dare
                                                    linger there!

His hounds run baying like wailing ghosts among ferns
                                                    and trees –
   From dusk till dawn you'll hear the forlorn
   Unearthly blowing of his hunter's horn;
           And whoever sees
The ragged antlers that grow out of his skull, is his to
                                                    seize!

Though hanged in the reign of Henry the Eighth, he's
                                                    hunting still
   On a huge black mare whose nostrils flare
   Phantoms of mist on the cold night air,
           For he's out to kill
As he storms through the land like a Demon, up and
                                                    downhill!

And deep in Windsor Forest, with the low clouds
scudding by,
On a winter's night by dim starlight
Herne the Hunter will heave into sight,
And you will surely die –
For you'll never shake off his spectral hounds,
however hard you try!

Night Visitor

What is it that taps at my window pane
   with a tap so light?
Neither twig nor leaf nor drift of rain
   wakes you this night.

It must be the wind, the wandering wind
   that prowls out there!
Neither wind nor breeze will you find
   in the still night air.

It must be some creature, mouse or bat,
   that's scratching away!
Neither mouse nor bat makes a sound like that
   by night or day.

Is it my dead friend's ghost that comes
   to wish me well?
No, it's not your dead friend's ghost that roams
   so far from Hell.

Then is it my enemy's ghost out there
   at my window-sill?
Yes, your old enemy's ghost, come to declare
   how I hate you still!

Etiquette

That snobbish medium, Lord Fitz-Pugh,
Wrote *The Departed Spirits' Who's Who*,
For he thought it ill-bred
To talk with the dead
Unless *they* were Somebody, too!

A Country Grandmother

My grandmother was famous for her hearing.
In the dead of night, when the whole village slept,
wrapped in the silence of moon and starlight,
not a cat in the market place, nor a solitary owl's
blank stare from the ivied tree trunk,
she alone, while my grandfather snored beside her,
would hear the knocking – always three sharp raps –
which came as warning from the Other Side
that someone close at hand would shortly die.

Quite often someone did.

The night she heard three raps three times repeated,
she roused my grandad, tidied up the house,
took the insurance policies from their secret place,
sat by the fender in the rocking-chair
and died with the first glimmer of the dawn.

Pillicock Hill

It's sixty years since Tom Turnbull and I
    climbed past the birch wood up Pillicock Hill,
with the ribbon of road unwinding below us
    and the farms and the houses death-still.

It's sixty long years since we flopped on the hillside,
    my best friend, Tom Turnbull, and I,
tired and laughing, not a care in the world,
    with the sun sinking low in the sky.

And it's sixty long years since I woke to find
    Tom Turnbull was gone from the hill;
and never did there blow from the horn of the moon
    a wind emptier or more chill.

It's sixty years since, but I knew without telling
    they could ransack till Kingdom Come
farmhouse and cottage, byre and barn,
    and find never one trace of Tom.

Sixty years ago, Tom Turnbull could outwhistle
    a dozen blackbirds at will,
and the tune he would whistle, time and again,
    was 'The Ferlie of Pillicock Hill'.

And for sixty years, though he's never been seen,
      when the moon's horned and everything's still,
faint as gnats' thin wailing, that same tune's come
      trailing
      from the dungeons of Pillicock Hill.

A Strangler's Hand

It's happening now, as it did once before,
    but this time, it's come to settle some score.
The simple fact is, that what's opened the door
    is a grave-spotted hand, and not a thing more!

No arm, and no body – just a leathery hand
    that comes groping towards me where I stand,
with the air freezing all around it, and
    the fear of it fills my mouth like dry sand.

I'd feel a bit easier if only it grew
    from the arm and the body of . . . no matter-who!
And my terror might slacken, if only I knew
    what it is the grim horror is trying to do.

Now it's inches away, and it just seems to float,
    and it's flexing its fingers to come at my throat,
but rather than strike, it just hangs there to gloat,
    while I cringe rabbit-like from the pounce of a
        stoat!

To be a Ghost

To be a ghost
it helps if you're able
to moan pitifully
like the night wind
in the tormented wood,
and can whine in chimneys,
wail down corridors,
bump and thump about
and rattle chains
in distant dungeons.

To be a ghost
it helps to have
a mouldering churchyard,
a monk's robes and hood
and a grinning skull,
dark shadows of yew trees
and a ruined abbey
with screech-owls flitting
through spectral moonlight
as midnight chimes.

These are the stock-in-trade
the public demands,
without which no claim
to be a ghost
can be considered serious.

But truly to be a ghost
what you need is
to be locked without hope of escape
in a time and place
and suffering
that not even centuries
can change; and of course
you must be dead.
But you mustn't know it!

And I Wait Patiently!

I am the ghost that troubles you most –
    the ghost you never can see,
though I'm always there on the shadowy stair
    or anywhere else you may be;
       and I wait patiently!

I am the shade of whom you're afraid –
    the ghost you never can hear,
and yet I *am* heard, though I don't say a word
    (or anything else) in your ear;
       and you seize up with fear!

I am the spirit you dread to the limit –
    the ghost you never can know;
I'm the sickening feeling that sets your heart reeling
    in fear of some unseen blow;
       but you can't turn and go!

I am the ghoul, clinging close as your soul –
    the ghost you never can find,
who wails without pause down the dark corridors
    of the prison you call your mind,
       where you stumble round, blind!

To be a Witch

To be a witch
you don't have to be old;
you don't need a hooked nose
studded with warts,
an eye bulging with evil,
and long skinny fingers.
You don't even need
munching gums
and a turned-up chin.

To be a witch
you don't need a cloak,
a tall cone hat,
a moon and a flying broomstick,
or a cauldron bubbling
with toads, deadly nightshade
and adder's tongue.
You don't need a raven
or so much as a cat.

To be a witch
you can love pop, discos,
skin-tight jeans,
and be blonde as snow.

All you really need
to be a witch
is a taste for cruelty,
a strong will
and a heart hard and cold as ice.

Mushroom Gatherers

The white witch comes with the crack of dawn,
      basket over one arm,
her feet disturbing the meadow dew –
      no cause for alarm!

Milkcap, puffball, blewit and cep,
      ink-cap, chanterelle;
witch's butter, honey fungus,
      horn of plenty and morel!

The black witch comes with the misty moon,
      basket over one arm,
her feet leave no trace in field or wood –
      and she means harm!

Panther cap, death cap, slimy beech tuft,
      yellow and red russula;
apple canker, stinkhorn, candle-snuff,
      destroying angel and sickener!

Witches' Laughter

I passed a dozen
Witches in a coven

All hunched and black
Beckoning me back

I bolted half-blind
Not looking behind

A skirl of laughter
Kept coming after

Like thorns that cackle
And blaze and crackle

Under a hot
Black cooking-pot

Cure for the Evil Eye

An evil eye can sour milk,
turn good luck to bad,
inflict disaster or disease
and, at the worst, kill.

To ward off the evil
you may cross your fingers,
spit twice on the ground
and carry in your pocket
coal, garlic or nutmeg;
or better still, shark's teeth
and a rabbit's paw.

But if what you seek
is a permanent cure,
empty your pockets,
hold all eyes with your own,
and treat with total contempt
all such unholy nonsense.

When You Were Ill

When you were ill in times gone by
the village witch would often try
to cure you of your aches and pains
by wandering off down country lanes.

> *Ragwort, comfrey, tormentil,*
> *goutweed, yarrow and crane's-bill.*

Bent in a hoop over her pot
sometimes she cured you, sometimes not;
but by her art a witch would strive
to see that you were kept alive.

> *Thistle, moon daisy, columbine,*
> *fleabane, nightshade and celandine.*

The doctor, on the other hand,
despised such means and took his stand
on scientific skills, whereby
he guaranteed that you would die.

> *Leech, knife, limbeck, blood –*
> *tapped, or drained, or in a flood!*

Hallowe'en Party

Go on, have fun, duck
your head, jab wide-jawed
at the floating apples
with teeth kept strong and white
by brushing and the dentist.
Get soaked as much as you like.

But after the party,
when the last slab of cake's eaten
and you've finished shuddering
with fear and delight
at spooky stories, when
the candles splutter and smoke
and quench messily in lanterns
of turnip and pumpkin, take off
your mask and, as you're driven
safely home by car, spare a thought
for the spent pain and sadness
of those old women, toothless
or with brown stumps of teeth,
who ate what they could out of hedges
and, if they were lucky enough
not to be ducked and drowned,
died uncomplaining in their lampless hovels.

The Wizard's Burial

At his burial, out on St Bees Head,
The St Bees Wizard turned restless and said,
As he sprang from the coffin
They'd carried him off in,
'The fact is, I don't *like* being dead!'

The Conjuror

He magicked a spider,
He magicked a bat,
He magicked two doves
That flew out of his hat.

I said, 'But that's small stuff!'
He tried once again,
But all that he magicked
Was a bantam hen.

I looked down my nose.
'Do you call that *big*?' –
He puffed and he strained
And he magicked a pig.

'That's more like it!' I said.
'But I've seen an old witch
Magic whales as big
As a football pitch!

'*You* couldn't magic a
Small tiger,' I bet him.
But he *did*. – And to prove it
The tiger ATE HIM!

Extra-sensory Perception

Investigating ESP,
Professor Poppleton, D.Sc.,
locked a medium in an empty room
sealed off, like an Egyptian tomb.
'Now then,' he intercomed, 'if it's true
you can conjure Something from Nothing, *do*
go right ahead. We'll be watching you!'

The medium, sneering at the prof,
stepped through a brick wall and pushed off,
leaving behind him as a clue
to just what ESP can do
a massive pot of plants (perennials),
a dozen doves, two yapping spaniels,
Houdini (handcuffed) and Paul Daniels!

The Magic Box

A poor farmer, ploughing his field one day,
churned up a large black box which he cleaned of clay
and set on the kitchen table. His good wife,
who'd owned nothing so fine in her whole life,
placed in it a single apple. Later, she
lifted the lid, and what then did she see
but a box brimful of apples, every one
exactly like the first! After she'd run
to fetch her husband, they munched and chewed
apples that were immediately renewed
each time they took one out! By selling them, they
were able to live in comfort, till one day
the farmer dropped a coin by accident
into the box, at which the apples went
and gold coins took their place; and when he tried
taking them out, the gold coins multiplied!
Soon, then, both farmer and wife were millionaires,
though now their new-found wealth imposed new
      cares:

46

the farmer's grandfather lived with the couple
(his breath came short, his old limbs were unsupple)
and they were furious he should be so slow
scooping out coins to make their fortune, so
one day it happened that the old man died,
working too hard. His body toppled inside
the box, at which the coins all disappeared,
and where they'd been, dead grandfathers upreared!
Now since by law all corpses were to be given
expensive funerals, the farmer was soon driven
into poverty burying dead grandfathers; then
the box, breaking in two, left him poor as when
he'd first found it; and he's a poor farmer again!

Never Since Eden

The Thing that came from Outer Space
And landed in the Jones' backyard
Had neither colour, size nor shape,
But a smell that caught us all off guard.

Never since Eden had there been
So sweet, so rich, so good a smell:
The neighbours, sniffing, gathered round
Like thirsting cattle at a well.

Never since Adam first kissed Eve
Had humans looked upon each other
With such joy that old enemies
Threw loving arms round one another.

One whiff, and babies stopped their crying,
And all the gossip was kind and good,
And thieves and thugs and hooligans
Danced in the street in holiday mood.

Old scores were settled with a smile,
And liars changed to honest men,
And the ugliest face was beautiful,
And the sick and infirm were made whole again.

The Thing that came from Outer Space
Purred like a cat at the heart of the smell,
But *how* it did, and *why* it did,
Was more than the Scientists could tell.

They roped it off, they cleared the streets,
They closed upon it, wearing masks,
Ringed it with Geiger counters, scooped
And sealed it in aseptic flasks.

They took it back to analyse
In laboratories white and bare,
And they proved with burette and chromatograph
That nothing whatever was there.

They sterilized the Jones' backyard
(The smell whimpered and died without trace),
Then they showed by mathematics that no Thing
Could have landed from Outer Space.

So the neighbours are quite their old selves now,
As loving as vipers or stoats,
Cheating and lying and waiting their chance
To leap at each other's throats.

The Swaffham Pedlar

(A supernatural dream)

A pedlar from Swaffham was plagued by a dream
that he stood on London Bridge, in the stream
of a jostling throng, for the bridge was then
lined with shops, stalls, houses, so that river-men,
shepherds and drovers, sheep, cattle and geese
swarmed over it day and night, without cease;
and a voice in his dream said that if he stood
patiently there, after a while he would
have the best news he'd ever hear in his life.
Tormented by this same dream, he kissed his wife
goodbye, took his small savings, and made his way
to the great city, walking the livelong day,
and sleeping by night in fields of new-mown hay.
At last, far from home, the pedlar from Swaffham
  found
himself in the middle of London Bridge, swirled round
by a shouting throng; but never a voice
brought him news that could cause his heart to rejoice.
A day dragged slowly by – a week. In the end,
hungry, with barely a penny to spend
on his last crust, he reflected he'd made
a prize fool of himself, and so, dismayed,
was gathering up his poor belongings to
go back home, when a curious shopkeeper drew
him to one side, and said: 'Sir, I'm puzzled by
your behaviour. Could you explain to me why
you've taken root, as it were, on this same spot,
since you don't beg or sell, and clearly you're not

a pickpocket?' Sheepishly, the pedlar spoke
of his dream, at which the shopkeeper broke
into wild fits of laughter. 'Sir, it would seem
you're nincompoop enough to believe a dream!
Everyone dreams, though surely no one but you
would ever believe such nonsense could prove true!
Why, I myself had a dream, only last night,
that if I found a place called Swaffham, I might
dig up a hoard of treasure long-since buried
in a poor pedlar's garden! – Now, if I hurried
off, spade in hand, to dig up some pedlar's oak,
wouldn't *you* laugh, and think the whole thing a huge
    joke,
worse even than buying a pig in a poke?'

As you'll guess, the pedlar, who let no grass grow
under his feet till he reached home, wasn't slow
to dig from the oak's root a fine treasure-chest
which not only made him rich for the rest
of his life, but gave him the chance to repair
the old parish church of Swaffham, which is where
you'll find his monument still, should you go there.

The First Banana Tree

Deep in the forest, gathering firewood,
Maria, lovelier than a fawn,
met an *anito*, but thought him human
and loved him dearly as ever woman
loved man, since glimmer of earth's first dawn.

The starlit night was not more tender,
nor moonlight silvering the palmed shore
more radiant than the *anito*'s eyes;
but love from a spirit of the skies
cannot stay earthbound evermore.

Maria scolded, wept and pleaded,
pitched to her knees and seized his hands,
vowing she'd never set him free
till stars and moon turned fish of the sea
and the hilltops skipped on the sands.

He looked his last look on Maria,
the fairest of all womankind,
then vanished in a blaze of light;
but through it all she held so tight
his hands that they were left behind.

She buried and watered them with her tears
till the damp earth heaved and before her eyes
a strange tree grew out of that strange root
with hands and bent fingers for its fruit;
gold gifts of a god from the skies.

anito: a supernatural sky spirit.

Old Man, Mumbling

What was it he muttered, Daft Davy,
ignoring the throng
of fair, market, football-ground,
mouthing and mumbling and wailing,
with the shreds of his overcoat trailing
his patched boots as he shuffled along?

He made no more sense than the sound
of autumn wind in the leaves
or the gurgling of rain in a gutter
or the brawling of birds in the eaves,
and he'd stammer and spatter and splutter
like a quarrel of wind and rain
debating their age-old argument
time and again.

For his talk was of God's poor creatures
all locked out of doors,
and of skies exploding and falling
on the mountains and moors,
and ruinous torrents of poison poured
down river and drain,
and golden harvests blown to dust
by the wild whirlwind, red as rust,
and a blinding blizzard of pain.

All nonsense! And yet, there were those who said
he'd some kind of second sight –
some lost instinct, by which he was led –
and, as a cat can see in the night,
so he could see in broad daylight
to walk and talk with the Dead!

★

'And do you walk with the Dead, Davy?
    And do you talk with the Dead?'
'And if I do, they're more real than you,'
    was all Davy said.

Remote Control
(Mind over matter)

In the playground, Mrs Jones
    Keeps an eagle eye
On kids in corners, kids that shout,
Kids that throw their weight about,
    Kids that scream and cry.

In the playground, Mrs Jones
    Never seems to see
How, when the kids stampede and race,
Everything that's taking place
    Is controlled by Bill and me.

In the playground, Mrs Jones
    Hasn't the least clue
That kids are stars that shoot and fall
And swim through space, and that they all
    Do what we tell them to.

In the playground, Mrs Jones,
    Blinded by her stare,
Thinks the two of us are nice and quiet,
Not knowing we can cause a riot
    Any time we care!

In the playground, Mrs Jones
    Doesn't even guess
She's in our power, and all she does
Is what we let her do, because
    We don't want any mess.

In her innocence, Mrs Jones
    Stares but cannot see
That the whole playground's one big sky
Of stars that flare and fade and die,
    Controlled by Bill and me.

Bill McQuire's Angel

We were gathered for Assembly
    in the rickety school hall,
with Miss Bramble at the piano,
    teachers, Headmaster and all.

No – not quite all, since Bill McQuire
    was either truanting or late;
but being neck-high in trouble seemed
    poor Bill McQuire's fate.

The Head stepped up to the platform
    and stared the murmuring down,
then, coughing to announce the hymn number,
    his face darkened in a frown.

For there at the back Bill McQuire
    came slap through the swing door
with one hand held up for attention,
    and the hubbub started once more.

'Quiet!' the Head called from the platform.
    'Well then, McQuire, what is it?'
'Please, sir, there's an angel in the school yard,
    come to pay us a visit.'

'Silence!' the Head roared, clenching his fists.
    'Go straight to my office, McQuire.
After Assembly, I'll teach you just what
    it means to be a liar.'

'Oh, but he's *not*!' – Miss Bramble had crossed
    to stand at the window where,
craning to look in the school yard, she
    could just glimpse an angel there.

'We'll return to the playground,' the Head said,
    and added, sarcastically:
'If an angel's come to visit us
    we'd better *all* go and see!'

So back we trooped to a school yard
    empty and blank as the sky,
while the Head kept snorting his anger,
    and Miss Bramble started to cry.

'Just where *is* the angel?' the Head jeered,
    with a mocking glance all round. –
Then the roof caved in and flattened the hall
    and the Head's voice was drowned.

The Closed School

Under the silvering light of the cold, tall sky,
Where the stars are like glimmering ice and the moon
    rides high,
Bolted and locked since the war by long-dead hands,
Next to the shadowy church, the closed school stands.

A village school, in the grip of frost and the past,
Its classrooms airless as tombs, its corridors waste;
Behind boarded windows barely an insect crawls
On the spreading atlas that is staining ceiling and
    walls.

Here is the stillness of death. Listen hard as you can,
There's not one sound to be heard that is noisier than
The creeping of mould, or the crumbling of masonry
Into a fine floor-dust, soft and powdery.

Only deeper than silence, at the far end of listening,
Come the feet in the corridors, silver voices that ring
In the raftered hall, and outside, where the frost
    freezes hard,
Brittle laughter of children snowballing in the yard.

Midnight Wood

Dark in the wood the shadows stir:
  What do you see? –
Mist and moonlight, star and cloud,
Hunchback shapes that creep and crowd
    From tree to tree.

Dark in the wood a thin wind calls:
  What do you hear? –
Frond and fern and clutching grass
Snigger at you as you pass,
    Whispering fear.

Dark in the wood a river flows:
  What does it hide? –
Otter, water-rat, old tin can,
Bones of fish and bones of a man
    Drift in its tide.

Dark in the wood the owlets shriek:
  What do they cry? –
Choose between the wood and river;
Who comes here is lost for ever,
    And must die!

Poisoned Talk

Who killed cock robin?
I, said the worm,
I did him great harm.
He died on the branch of a withered tree
From the acid soil that poisoned me.

Who killed the heron?
I, mouthed the fish,
With my tainted flesh
I killed tern, duck and drake,
All the birds of the lake.

Who killed the lake?
I, boasted Industry,
I poisoned with mercury
Fish, plant and weed
To pamper men's greed.

Who killed the flowers?
I, moaned the wind,
I prowl unconfined,
Blowing acid rain
Over field, flood and fen.

Who killed the forest?
I ensured that it died,
Said sulphur dioxide,
And all life within it,
From earthworm to linnet.

Two Rivers

Says the River Till to the River Tweed:
  You hurtle by at twice my speed,
but what's the good of that to you
  when I drown so many, and you so few?

Says the River Tweed to the River Till:
  It's true enough that you run still
but drown many more than ever I do –
  and what I say is MORE SHAME ON YOU!

Phantom Spitfire

In the dead of night, in clear moonlight,
        a distant hum grows shrill
as a phantom Spitfire zooms into sight
        just south of Biggin Hill,
and there it will race across its old base,
        tilting in perfect control,
as it used to do during World War Two,
        in a low victory roll.

The Bell Beneath the Sea

When, far from the shore, the dark waves roar
       in a wild commotion,
on the rising swell a wrecked ship's bell
       tolls deep, deep in the ocean.

No one knows who tolls for the long-drowned souls
       in the cavernous sea,
but they hear the spell of the phantom bell
       and rise up, silently.

It is then that they roam like fiends on the foam
       and drag to the ocean floor,
as the watery bell clangs a grim death-knell,
       sailors who'll never sail more!

Phantom Schooner

Last night as we were sailing
    beyond the Hebrides,
A Phantom Schooner crossed our bows
    and tacked in heavy seas,
and hailed us through the whistling wind,
    which caused our blood to freeze.

Us old 'uns knew to shut our eyes
    and turn our heads away;
but the young 'uns laughed and hailed it back,
    taking it all for play;
and every last one of them dropped dead
    before the break of day!

The Merchildren's Complaint

There are numerous stories of Mermaids
With long hair as yellow as straw,
Leaving their deep-sea grottoes
For love of a sailor on shore.

Everybody feels sorry for Mermen,
With their hearts full of grief and devotion,
Weeping for love of the wives they've lost
And adding more salt to the ocean.

But whoever mentions *Merchildren*?
Doesn't anyone make a fuss
That our mums swim off, and our dads just weep,
And there's no one to care about *us*?

> They sing songs about our mums,
> They tell tales about our dads –
> So why aren't there songs and tales about
> Us *Merlasses* and *Merlads*?

Unicorn

Of all earth's creatures, none
is so difficult to kill
as the pure white unicorn.

Even the crusaders
failed to bring back more
than remnants of his carcass –
hide, hooves, mane, but chiefly
the convoluted lance
of his single magical horn.
Supreme among beasts,
a fair match even for the lion,
his dwelling is mountain-tops
and waste desert lands;
but so fierce is he,
no hunter dare come near him.

According to old books
the only certain way
to kill a unicorn
is to use the bait
of a beautiful girl
who's roped to a tree
and left to weep there;
then, when the unicorn comes,
made gentle by her beauty,

to sleep at her feet, head
lowered pityingly
in her lap, killing him
is simple as cutting
butter with a knife.

It is precisely
because beautiful girls
resent being roped to trees
and have, besides good looks,
the sheer good sense
to be animal-lovers,
that to this day
the unicorn remains
an unendangered species
and is, of all earth's creatures,
the most difficult to kill.

Bunyips

Bunyips are maned, Australian creatures
      of prodigious size:
eel-like, but with kangaroo features
      and hypnotic eyes.

You'll find them in the outback where
      whole families of them throng
by lake and inlet or somewhere near
      a stream or billabong.

If seen, they are intent on slaughter
      and fix you with a stare
that brings you walking across water
      straight into their lair.

A mother Bunyip has a glower
      that's very like a Devil,
and by this means she has the power
      to raise the water level.

And if you're fool enough to let
      that water lap upon
your shoes or boots or naked feet,
      you'll turn into a swan!

From the Horse's Mouth

It was dusk as I strolled down a country lane
When a voice from nearby spoke plain as plain:

Did you know I won the Derby in seventy-three?
Yet when I turned round there was no one to see!

The fields stretched empty as the shadowy air
But for one old horse that was grazing there.

So on I walked down the darkening lane
When the same voice spoke, and said over again:

Did you know I won the Derby in seventy-three?
And when I looked, that horse was following me!

So I took to my heels, like a shot from a gun –
Three desperate miles to the Rising Sun.

I'd no breath to speak with, as I fell through the door,
But they helped me as if they'd seen all this before.

'You've no need to explain,' the landlord said
as he drew me a pint, and shook his grey head.

'That old horse tells more lies than have ever been
    reckoned.
It was seventy-*two*, and the beast came *second*!'

Death Came Stalking

Death came stalking through the town
and swore that he'd take Mr Brown;
but first he seized on Mr Black
and simply *wouldn't* hand him back!
Next day, he erred again, and chose
to carry off young Mr Rose;
then pounced (trying to set things right)
on unsuspecting Mr White –
and even after *that* was seen
throttling that nice man, Mr Green!
Ashamed at last, he slunk away,
taking with him Mr Grey.

'It's just not *fair*,' their widows whined,
'that Death should be so colour-blind!'

Homecoming

Suddenly water, loud in the dark,
        came lapping the shore,
and I dragged a boat clear of the sedge
        and took up an oar
and rowed on the starless waters till,
        weary, I rowed no more.

Light filtered through the dark and mist
        from a house I'd known
in dreams since my childhood, its terrace
        and walls overgrown
with magnolia and lichen and moss;
        and I stood there alone.

And I groped as I'd groped in my dreams
        to push the door wide
on the silent, familiar faces
        that waited inside
nodding their slow, stately welcome –
        and I knew I had died!

Passing the Churchyard

As I walked past the churchyard
    in the silvery light of dawn,
I heard a shivering voice complain:
    'It's cold at the roots of the thorn!'

As I passed again the churchyard
    with the sunlight full on me,
came a doleful whisper: 'How dark it is
    at the roots of the cypress tree!'

And as I passed the churchyard
    in the glimmer of twilight's dew,
a sad voice wavered at my ear:
    'It's lonely at the roots of the yew!'

But at midnight in the churchyard
    with the moon high overhead,
thorn and cypress and yew cast their shadows,
    and never a word was said!

City Churchyard

In their narrow beds, under hunched headstones,
the dead continually talk, huddled in families,
with friends and old enemies in mounds beyond.

Being dead, their only voices are wind and rain.

By day, their talk is drowned too deep for hearing
in the boom of traffic. Only in the dead hours of night
do their borrowed voices come into their own,
whispering and whimpering among grass and
    trembling leaves,
gurgling in gutters when the black rain falls,
or moaning their pain on biting winter winds.

What is it that they say? – They say what the
    chattering stars say,
scattering like geese across freezing skies till dawn.

Grave Talk

As I walked down the churchyard
    I heard a dead man say,
'Is that my old friend, Stephen,
    That's passing by this way?'

Now you might think a dead man's voice
    Would fill the heart with dread,
But if Tom never hurt me, living,
    What harm should he do me, dead?

'Ay, Tom, it's Stephen, right enough.
    I keep your memory green,
For it's many a time I've missed you
    Since you died last Hallowe'en!'

'Ah, if only you knew how often
    I've summoned you, as you've passed;
But now you hear me, rest assured
    All will be well at last!'

'But how is it I can hear you now,
    When I never heard you before?'
'Friend Stephen, there are mysteries
    You'd do better to ignore!'

'But tell me – how and where are you?
        And do you rot in clay?
Or are you fed, and clothed and shod
        In a far brighter day?'

'Spare me your questions, Stephen, then I
        Need tell you no lies!'
'But are you in Purgatory or Hell,
        Or perhaps Paradise?'

'Hush and be patient, my good old friend! –
        The mysteries you would know
Will be yours to keep for ever
        By tomorrow's cock-crow!'

Success at Last

Here in this vault lies Ffitch-Wren Ffitch-Wren,
Who did everything over and over again.
He took three or four baths in an average day
And shaved so often his chin wore away,
While the only meals that ever he tasted
Were three good breakfasts – lunch and dinner were
    wasted!
When he came to marry, he did it by fives,
And was five times divorced from his five wives,
Leaving five sons behind him: Ffitch-Wren, and again,
Ffitch-Wren and Ffitch-Wren and Ffitch-Wren and
    Ffitch-Wren.
He stumbled and st-stammered and was thought a
    great dunce –
But success came at last, and he died only once!

Epitaph on a Prophet

Here lies the prophet, Nathaniel Sly,
the loneliest man in the Isle of Skye,
who, whenever you met him, would solemnly sigh
and tell you (looking you straight in the eye)
just *where*, *how* and *when* you are going to die!

Epitaph

Here lie I, Jock Featherstone,
the seventh son of a seventh son,
who was born and died on a Hallowe'en
and made a living in between
by telling fortunes, good and ill;
and in my grave I keep my skill,
and warn whoever reads this verse
to pray for my soul, or carry my curse.
Whosoever dares damage this stone
will die the same night the deed is done,
for I, Jock Featherstone, the Wizard,
shall come in the dark and slit his gizzard!

The Billy James Story

We've got a ghost on our estate,
a ghost that's really up-to-date –
not like the spooks of long ago
who moan and groan and come and go,
flitting around in fancy dress
to find somebody to distress.

We went to school with Billy James.
He talked like us; he shared our games;
he chatted the girls up in the caf
and did mad things to make you laugh,
especially when Sally Blair
happened (by chance?) to be in there;
and when he joined the Army he
was no different from you or me.

We never dreamed we'd hear Billy's name
on television, but it came
bang at the start of *News at Ten*:
'Eighteen years old' . . . 'his next of kin
have been informed' . . . 'the IRA' . . .
what the Prime Minister had to say.

What with three bullets lodged in his chest,
you'd think that Billy James might rest,
but Billy had his whole life to live
and never was the sort to give
in easily; and I tell you straight,
the ghost that hangs round our estate
is the saddest ghost you'll ever see,
whether he's standing silently
under the street-lamp, near her door,
in a blood-stained tunic, waiting for
a glimpse of Sally, or sitting where
he used to sit, with a frozen stare,
in the far corner of the caf;
and we remember how he'd laugh,
knowing he'll never laugh again,
for what he feels, he can't explain,
and we can't reach or ease his pain.

Seance

I

It was midnight on the housing estate
and a few teenagers were staying up late
to drink a few cans, when the talk turned to spooks
amid cheers and jeers, and some knowing looks
from Katie, who scribbled the alphabet
on bits of paper she carefully set
with a tumbler on the table-top. So,
gathered round, they scoffed at the YES and NO
she placed at each end: 'Kate, what'll the spook say
when we ask "Are you there?" and it's gone away?' –
But the answer came back YES, even after
they'd stopped their cheating and clowning, and the
    laughter
died down to the creepy silence of a tomb.
'What'll I ask it?' Katie said, and the room
grew suddenly cold, and their fingers froze
on the upturned glass. – 'Ask it what no one knows!'
Tom kept on whispering. But what could that be?
'Ask it to tell the future,' begged Anne-Marie,
who hadn't a boy. Then Fred shot to his feet:
'Got it! Let's fix it so that it can't cheat!'
(Fred knew all about horses, and played them, too.)
'It's winter now, and there's nobody who
knows what the runners will be next Derby Day.
Just ask who'll win the Derby's what *I* say!' –
But already the glass was moving to spell,
letter by letter, the name: CHRISTABEL!

Months passed and all was forgotten when Fred
bought the *Sporting World* one morning and read
the list of Derby runners, and there, in it,
was – CHRISTABEL, and a dead cert to win it
with odds (incredibly) of forty to one!
So what they all did was what *you*'d have done:
ignored the fact that the whole thing was spooky,
sold the shirts off their backs to pay the bookie,
and mad with excitement, wished their life away,
in desperate longing for Derby Day.

III

Like hunched witches watching their cauldron bubble,
on Derby Day they were all of a huddle
round Fred's TV, where they saw CHRISTABEL
leave the starting-post like a bat out of Hell
and romp clear ahead of the rest of the field
(their hearts drummed drunkenly; their senses reeled)
when CHRISTABEL, pushed to the uttermost,
collapsed twenty yards from the finishing-post,
turned up a round belly, and gave up the ghost!

Everywhere

Everywhere I cast my eye
Groans of shadows, walls that sigh;
The tall, cracked mirror's piercing cry.

Everywhere I lean my ear
Shadows that flounder and uprear
Like scrambling bats as I draw near.

Everywhere I place my foot
Horror of its taking root
In shadows thickening into soot.

Everywhere I turn my head
Damp smells of grief; the noiseless tread
And soundless sniggering of the dead.

Everywhere I turn to leave
Webbed emptinesses cling and cleave.
Their clammy sorrows pluck my sleeve.

The Loogaroo

His horse's flanks scarred by sharp fangs,
   legs trembling, eyes bulged with fear . . .
The old Stableman needs no second look:
it's as plain to him as an open book
   that the foul Loogaroo was here!

He melts down a bright dollar-piece
   to a silver bullet; hides,
gun in hand, in the hay-loft; watches and waits.
Day dims; night wakes; pale moonlight penetrates
   the shadowed silence on all sides.

Dead of night, and a strange donkey comes –
   black, bristling, its stench like a sty –
to sink its fanged teeth in the shuddering flesh
of a horse that uprears, neck strained, hooves athresh,
   as its life's blood's sucked and drained dry.

The Stableman takes good aim and fires.
   The Loogaroo, wounded, bounds
whinnying into the night, leaving a spoor
of blood that ends at Mr De Groos's door.
   The Stableman hides in the grounds.

A doctor's car, soon followed by
   an ambulance! – But he
steals home; says never a word; for who'd choose
to think ill of respectable Mr De Groos,
   famed for his wealth and charity?

The weeks drag by. Mr De Groos
 returns to his home once more,
then, propped on crutches, makes his first visit to
the house of his neighbour the Stableman, who
 hardly dares to open the door.

'Not a single soul have I told,'
 the old Stableman pleads.
'Nor I,' says De Groos, 'but I thought I'd call.
I'd an accident cleaning my gun, that's all –
 let's be friends and forget old misdeeds!'

The Stableman can't believe his luck.
 De Groos holds out his hand:
'Let's shake on it!' – But before he can pull it
away, the Stableman feels a hard bullet
 press into his palm like a brand.

'Take back what's yours, though dug from my flesh,'
 jeers De Groos, and turns to go
from the Stableman, who's tormented by itches
and a rash that pains worse the more he scratches,
 till it covers him, head to toe.

That same night, under a storm-blown moon,
 his body bristles black;
feet and hands harden in hooves, teeth sharpen to
blood-hungry fangs, and he's turned Loogaroo,
 with the foul fiend humped on his back.

Loogaroo: West Indian for a man who takes on an animal
form at night to do the Devil's work.

Branch-Line Ghost

I

It was, as I remember,
a dark midnight in November
when I dashed for the last train
through blank fog and seeping rain.
As I opened the train door
the train lurched and pitched me spraw-
ling – arms and flaying feet –
headlong on the carriage seat
where, straightening up, I found
blood on my forehead. Looking round
the carriage, empty and ill-lit
like a mobile tomb as it
click-clacked down the old branch line,
I saw the shadows re-combine
into a ghostly wild-eyed guard
facing me, and breathing hard.
My turn, then, to gasp and stare!
God's my witness, he wasn't there
when I lurched in. What's more,
these trains have no corridor!
Never have I felt such eyes
pierce me so and paralyse –
eyes that seemed to glow and gloat
as the scream died in my throat,
while my hands, raised up in prayer,
shook with horror in mid-air.

It appears that I passed out!
How, then, does it come about
that no one's found me lying
– Good heavens, I could be dying –
in this God-forsaken train;
and just how do you explain
there's no movement, sound or light –
just the dank smells of the night?
No one stirs and no one cares . . .
Could it be that no one dares
come and get me out of fear
that the ghost still lingers here –
and so abandons me to this
long nightmare of paralysis?

II

I came off duty just on half past ten
   and looked in at the Railway Inn
for something to keep out the fog and the damp
   that was numbing me under the skin.

Just after twelve I'd a word with Jim Hawkes
   (it's him drives the Twelve-O-Nine),
then I climbed in a carriage as dark as a cave
   to go home on the old branch line.

Well, the next thing I know, the train's pulling out
   and this geezer's swept off his feet
as he scrambles on board, and the train gives a jolt
   that spread-eagles him over the seat.

The minute I saw him I knew him for sure,
   with his spats and old-fashioned gear.
I cringed back in my seat, but his eyes picked me out,
   panting wildly and speechless with fear.

Those eyes were never the eyes of the living,
   for they held me like murderous chains,
while the screams seized up in my throat and the warm
   blood curdled to ice in my veins.

And there on his brow was his own blood, too,
   just a scarlet dribble, no more,
staining his high starched collar and drip-drip-drip-
   ing dark drops on the carriage floor.

He raised both his hands to strike me down – hands
    that shook with the anger of Hell –
then the train slowed climbing the gradient
    and I hurled myself clear as they fell.

It's easy to say I'd been drinking; that it
    all was a dream of some kind.
This plaster I'm wearing's for a broken neck. –
    Do you *still* think it's all in my mind?

Yes, I'd heard the old story, and I'll say it's all
    imagination, since you insist.
But just *what* are the bloodstains on the carriage floor?
    Poppies? Attar of roses? *Scotch mist?*

Ghost Village by the Shore

There's a village and a harbour where the tide groans
    night and day,
A place where trippers never come and where no
    children play
With the shifting, muddy sands that are silting up the
    bay.

And the village is half-empty and those who live there
    yet
Sit huddled by their fires as if trying to forget
All the sorrow of a lifetime and the ghosts for whom
    they fret.

For the harbour did not always lie abandoned, and the
    tide
Bore proudly once these boats that now lie rotting on
    their side,
And the laughing men who sailed in them were worth a
    nation's pride.

But when the grim night fell that struck them old at
    one swift blow,
Of all who nurse their sorrow in the crumbling village
    now
Not one had a streak of grey in her hair, or wrinkle on
    her brow.

All day before, the slate-grey sea heaved up at the
     slate-grey sky,
And the shore-bound fishermen mending their tackle
     watched with a wary eye
Where the tilting ocean fumed and foamed like a beast
     in agony.

And at twilight when the western clouds were stained
     as if with blood
The fishermen met in the Harbour Inn, and their
     leader spoke where he stood:
'We'll keep a watch tonight by turns, so sleep while the
     going's good.'

The wind howled round the shuttered inn, and tore
    down the sign where it hung.
And a short while they stayed to drink a tot, and a
    merry song was sung;
Then they suddenly went quiet as the tocsin bell was
    rung.

And white-faced in the dark they loosed their boats
    and let them slip
Into the sea's black torrent while, exploding like a
    whip,
The storm alive with lightning lashed and broke the
    sinking ship.

And lightning, too, revealed to those who knelt upon
    the shore
The sullen anger of the waves while for a time they
    bore
Young sweethearts, husbands, brothers, all straining
    at the oar.

And like a god, the ocean first took in his mighty hand
A score of men who in pure love defied his great
    command –
And in contempt he smashed them and the little boats
    they manned.

From the ship that went down not a man, not a rat got
    away,
And of those who went out in the dark, never one saw
    the day,
Though later the tide swept their bodies back into the
    bay.

There's a village and a harbour where the midnight
    tide still groans
For the brave men it has drowned, and with eyes as
    still as stones
The villagers lie waiting for the wind that stirs and
    moans.

For the wind, the wind comes drowning a merry song
    that's sung,
And it tears the creaking inn-sign from the place where
    it is hung,
And blows dead faces through the dark while the
    tocsin bell is rung.

A Souter's Greed
(The tale of a Border cobbler)

I

Before the cock had flapped its wings
    Or stretched its neck to crow
Came the clanging of the shop-bell
    Hung over the door below,
Which groaned on its tortured hinges
As the wind wrenched it to and fro.

The Souter's wife, she froze in her sleep;
    The Souter, nightcap on head,
At one stroke surfaced from dreams as dark
    And deep as an ocean-bed.
'I bolted and barred that door last night . . .
There's a thief broken in!' he said.

And first he fumbled for the tinder
    And next for the candlestick,
With hand a-tremble like the flame
    That smoked and writhed on its wick;
And his giant shadow crouched over him
On the stairs, and his breathing came thick.

The shop lay like a black well stirred
　　By gusts of cold night air,
And bits of it sprang to life, then died –
　　Bench, last, a hard-backed chair,
Hammer and pincers and coiling leather –
As he paused on the bottom stair.

He cupped the candle with his hand
　　And, 'Who's down there?' he said,
With face as white as his nightshirt,
　　Teeth rattling in his head . . .
'Over here!' boomed a voice among shadows,
Remote as a voice from the dead.

And a shadow stepped clear of the shadows
　　Into the trembling light,
Tall and black and spattered with mud.
　　'There's no need to take fright,
But' – glancing down at his own bare feet –
'I have urgent business this night!'

II

'Feet mottled and cold to the touch
      As any clay . . .'
'Here, drink your tot,' his Goodwife said,
      'For it's break of day.'

'Balanced his leg on this very stool . . .
      A gentleman bred . . .
Measure my foot, I'll come for my shoes –
      Ask what you like, he said.

'Gave me no name, nor yet address,
      But went at cock-crow . . .
A shadow that drifts among shadows
      Out there in the snow.'

'It's your brains are fuddled with sleep
      And dreams of the night;
Just make the gentleman's shoes, husband,
      And all will come right.'

And make them he did, of fine green leather,
      And set on a shelf.
'I'll take his gold,' the Souter swore, 'though
      It's Old Nick himself!'

III

Before the cock had flapped its wings
    Or stretched its neck to crow
The shop-bell clanged in the dark well
    Of the empty shop below
And the door groaned again on its hinges
As the wind wrenched it to and fro.

The Souter's wife opened one blear eye;
    The Souter lurched from his bed,
Fumbled for tinder and candlestick
    And stood trembling at the stair-head:
'Coming this very minute, Sir,
If you'll kindly but wait,' he said.

The Souter's pulse beat a wild tattoo,
    His eyes glittered with fright,
And his own huge shadow stalked him as
    He stole by candlelight
Downstairs, where the shadows staggered like bats
And the Stranger reared bolt upright.

He took from the shelf the fine leather shoes
    And never a word said he,
But knelt and shod each death-cold foot,
    Mottled as feet might be
After they'd rotted in some chill tomb
For a whole dead century.

Though fear had paralysed his tongue
    The Souter's hand unclasped,
And kneeling still, he lifted it,
    Begging and aghast;
For greed alone could have tamed such fear,
And his trembling hand still grasped!

And the Stranger thrust a purse in it,
    Heavy and wet as clay.
'I smell the dawn on the rising wind –
    Be warned by what I say!
Our bargain's done. Let my memory fade
As dreams fade in the blinding day!'

IV

The snow held the prints of the fine leather shoes
             To signpost his way
As the Souter slunk through the village street
             At break of day.

Not a neighbour stirred, not a chimney smoked;
             The cows watched untended
As he crossed the meadow to the grey churchyard
             Where the footprints ended.

Just a mouldering gravestone, blank from the slow
             Wear and tear of the years! –
And his heart's greed, a shrilling bugle to drown
             The voice of his fears.

A wild search for a spade, a frenzy of digging,
             A lid torn from its screws:
Then the Stranger, stretched in his coffin, still wearing
             His fine leather shoes!

V

'Husband, things aren't what they seem,
What you tell me's a bad dream.
Ghosts and graveyards, if you please –
All this comes from taking cheese
Late at night, and too much beer!'

'These are the very shoes, my dear . . .'

'*And* they've not been out of here!'

'Since you'll have it so, I must
Take you fully in my trust
(Break it, and you have my curse!).
Take and open, then, this purse . . .
Squeamish, are you? Mould and worm
Will not do you lasting harm.
Let your fingers grope and fold
Twenty guineas of pure gold!'

'Husband, you have been too bold –'

'Hush! Take care and guard your knowledge –
Save your breath to cool your porridge.'

'But the shoes!'

                  'Are mine to sell.'

'No, he more than paid you well;
Keep your bargain, as he said.'

'Fool! Who'd bargain with the dead?
I'll be busy, while you deplore.
Here's what he never bargained for –
Steel bolts, and new locks on the door!'

VI

Before the cock had flapped its wings
    Or stretched its neck to crow
A gale like a madman came howling
    Across fields of ice and snow
To wrench the roof from the Souter's house
And shatter the door at a blow.

A blizzard picked clean the bedroom of
    The fine shoes under the bed
And the earthy purse under the pillow
    And the Souter, nightcap on head;
But spared the Goodwife to tell her tale
Before she went mad, so it's said.

They found the gravestone, blank from the slow
    Wear and tear of the weather;
They dug and found in a stranglehold
    Souter and Stranger together –
This one clutching a purse still; the other
Wearing shoes of fine leather!

Index of First Lines